SHIRT IN HEAVEN

D1282502

Shirt in Heaven

* * *

Jean Valentine

Copper Canyon Press
Port Townsend, Washington

Copper Canyon Press is in residence at Fort Worden State
Park in Port Townsend, Washington, under the auspices
of Centrum. Centrum is a gathering place for artists and
creative thinkers from around the world, students of all
ages and backgrounds, and audiences seeking extraordinary
cultural enrichment.

LIBRARY OF CONGRESS CATALOGING-IN-PUBLICATION DATA
Valentine, Jean.
[Poems. Selections]
Shirt in heaven / Jean Valentine.
pages; cm
ISBN 978-1-55659-478-6 (softcover: acid-free paper)
I. Title.
PS3572.A39A6 2015
811'.54—dc23
2014031780

3 5 7 9 8 6 4 2
FIRST PRINTING

COPPER CANYON PRESS
Post Office Box 271
Port Townsend, Washington 98368

www.coppercanyonpress.org

for Emily Wilson
2002–2013
in loving memory

Contents

Luna Moth

Friend

Threshold

Then had we well put to,
without form, without text

SHIRT IN HEAVEN

Luna Moth

Luna Moth

Luna moth
at the black window

I hold you in my signal-memory
but I can't get back to how to talk to you,
silent as the black window.

Silent as your body
little book
on which
I in my hunger wrote.

A Child's Drawing, 1941

A woman ladder leans
with her two-year-old boy in her arms.
Her arms & legs & hands & feet
are thin as crayons.

The man ladder
is holding his glass of bourbon,
he is coming out of the child's drawing
in his old open pajamas—

he's in the war. The sky
is blackest crayon-canyon.
When does he leave again? When he leaves,
I leave.   I like that river the sky.

1943: The Vision

I saw it when I was nine
alone   looking into a shed

a human head   cut in two   lengthwise
in profile, lifelike, in a museum-size
glass jar, on a shelf.

I knew what it meant:
You must put the head back together again.

How could I put the head back together again?
But I promised. Everyone promised: dark eyes
to dark eyes.

Forest, Stars

Now the stars didn't show:
It was after the forest fire,

after her friend had lost his thinking
in the war— after

he had come upon a silence:
blood   saliva   semen   her

Her last year

Rest your mouth.
Rest your music.
Rest your walking around.   Sit down.
Drink.   Eat.

With my eyes, I see you eat stones.
I see you eat bones.
You eat mud. You eat the light.

I don't recognize anything.

Not a sign, a cut, a knife, a dark wood, a net.

I recognize everything.
The sign, the cut, the knife,
the dark wood, the net.

for Marina Tsvetaeva

God of rooms

God of rooms, of this room made of taken-away
papers and books, of removal, this single
room made of taken-away
empty now, god of empty rooms, god of
one unable to speak, god of turned-over boats
in the wind (god of boat and mouth and ear)
listen to someone, be of-you
needful to someone

for Paul Celan

Hold the finch

Hold the finch who flew into the window
till he can fly. But the window
flies into his face, over & over.

*

Send warm clothes,
send money.

Not knowing the last part
when or how would you die
—in want of

warm clothes, money,
for the last part

(no longer granted your friend)

*

She took her pocketbook,
her clothes, set out,
no company, no deeds,
a hoard of words.

*

Lie down, living human thought,
let your anxious glance like a house cat's glance
ask in its speechless rising and setting,
Do I concern you? Am I there?

for Osip & Nadezhda Mandelstam

1945

The winter trees offer no shade no shelter.
They offer wood to the family of wood.

He comes in at the kitchen door, waving like a pistol
a living branch in his hand, he shouts
"Man your battle stations!"

Our mother turns to the kitchen curtains.
He shakes the branch, a house-size Big Dipper

points north over the yard:
Can it help? How about

the old dog, thumping her tail. Whose dog is she?
How about the old furnace, breathing.

                                        Breathing the

world: a flier, a diver,
kitchen curtains, veterans, God, listen kindness,
we're in this thing like leaves.

For love,

you leapt sometimes
you walked away sometimes

that time on the phone you
couldn't get your breath
I leapt but couldn't get to you

I caught the brow that bid the dead
I caught the bough that hid

I'm, you know, still here,
tulip, resin, temporary—

Shirt in Heaven

Come upon a snapshot
of secret you, smiling like FDR, leaning on your crutches—

come upon letters I thought I'd burned—

I suppose you've got a place with lots of stairs.

I'm at the end of something, you're at the beginning.

I'd be rich, I'd get you an elevator:
a rare old smoky wood one.

I was at the beginning, so I was the oldest:
a looking-away door that opens at your touch.

      —dearest, they told me a surgeon sat down
in the hospital morgue, next to your body, & cried.
He yelled at the aide to get out.

His two sons had been your students
—me too, little-knowing—

there's nothing when

there's nothing when you're young and clare
but love and nowhere for it
for it to go but your
sweet open eye to the wounded
eye of the beloved
Then the bony aloneness
forty years &
forty years
and then   your eye again
& now we talketh all day long
& every night I keep my window
at your window   Yet my arms
get pulled out into   incomprehensible wind   Yet
you sweetly ask
in the silk wind
Will I come

Peace to bad waters

driftwood   seaweed
your sleeping arms, earthless
profile, drift,

Sleep, finished
here, bad waters, peace,
sadness drawn
across your mouth, peace

Bardo

You were picking through a trash bag,
taller than you.
Taking out anything worth something.

Our eyes met. I thought
What keeps us here? Two-legged?
You looked right through me.

My teacher says, just say to yourself,
Something will happen.
Something happen.

I could take off my clothes
and leave them on the ground,
I could walk off into the snow

out of human sight, out of

all the northern evening's gold brocade

W. 13th Street

I saw a table on the sidewalk
after snow   Candles,
wineglasses, a penciled note
Remember that I love you

Tall snow and the huddled cars.
The table like a car opening down.
I went down through, & I saw
a country picnic was prepared for you

who scree the dark canyon incognito
thin line of black hair you were born with, down your spine.

Open

I lay down under language
it left me and I slept

—You, the Comforter, came into the room
I moved my head—

my blood, my mouth
all buttoned away—

Makers of houses, books, clothes-
makers, goodbye—

A leaf, a shadow-hand

A leaf, a shadow-hand
blows over my head
from outside time
now & then
this time of year, September

—this happens—
—it's well known—
a soul locked away inside
not knowing anyone,
walking around, but inside:

I was like this once,
and you, whose shadow-hand
(kindness) just now blew over my head, again,
you said, "Don't ever think you're a monster."

You rope that pulls them where they do not go

horse running sideways
on only water

no school   no teacher   fire
made out of fire
poison houses

children in a rough line
holding onto a rope

a man with a cell phone pulling the rope
the reception breaking up

*

The man *had* to leave the books behind
Leave night behind   I know you don't use words there

sleepwalking a word-scrap   Day-walking my Redeem'

I'm lifting something very light   a blanket
Outside the window you're lifting something very heavy

Pat the rope then
chew the rope apart

I know you don't have teeth there
I know you don't have hands there

The helicopter,

The helicopter,
a sort of controlled silver leaf
dropped lightly into the clearing.
The searchlights swung, the little girl,
the little girl was crying, her mother, a girl herself,
was giving birth, the forest dropped birdseeds of milk.
Then the helicopter lifted away,
the mother rested.

        Like him who came to us empty-handed,
who came, it seemed, with nothing,
Joseph Cornell—   making
a shoebox universe to put it all in.

When I lost my courage

When I lost my courage and my thought
God still sat sewing by the window.
I threw myself to everywhere—
the harbors, everywhere
the poets & painters were.

The dancers—
misunderstandings
higher, deeper, colder—
but beauty—
but the lovers' curtained Dutch beds
over & over
sewn together & torn again—

His hand takes

His hand takes after me with a knife.
His blanked-out eye looks out   sharp
and does not like what it sees.   "Cunt."

        After everything there,
the tall Marys—most dearest cunts—
and little Keats rested in with me,
under the bridge of the lamplight—

Until day came, and the day driver.

Bury your money

Now, there: there's the money.

Great captivities tap
in our sleep.

But we made a promise   God and us
to meet in another life
when we both could want it.
If only one of us wanted, that
wouldn't be enough.
We made a promise to be naked
—though great famines bury the ear and the mouth,
though captivities cut parts away, or swell, or sap them,
we made a promise to be naked, John Cage said
Music is continuous; only listening is intermittent.

Poem with endwords by Reginald Shepherd

I saw it—there's
the bright snow—it's never
going to be enough
for this intimate world
—never enough for
the third strange angel, you.

She will be

She will be
a standing gong
struck from inside
that will go on sounding out
from her own stomach, no, *the*
little thumb-like object in her chest

it's making its sound
in her room
or in a desert someplace   sound-waves   my conscience
My conscience *knows*
its hurt   Most
strange & lucent thumb, told it

for Alice Notley

Friend

[The ship] is slowly giving up her sentient life.
I cannot write about it.

Shackleton, diary

Next to where their ship went down
they pitched their linen tents.

You, mountain-climbing,
mountain-climbing,
wearing your dead father's flight jacket—

My scalp is alive,
love touched it. My eyes are open water. Yours too.

Sitting in the dark Baltimore bar
drinking Coke
with you with your inoperable cancer
with your meds

no tent
no care what we look like
what we say

Later that night, in my room
looking into the mirror, to tell the truth I was loved.
I looked right through into nothing.

Hospice

I wore his hat
as if it was the rumpled coat
of his body, like I could put it on.

The coat of his hair, of his brain, its glitter
he gave it to me, something he'd worn.
He didn't touch his dog, touch was too much,

he didn't let her go.
I felt his hat on my head, like a hand,
though his hat was on the floor, just by my chair.

I went on drinking water
as if there was more water.
I went on living on earth
as if there was still life
on earth

      I remembered
like an islander   my island

like a calving iceberg, air

like jazz
rumpled
like its glitter
worn hand
by my chair

*

I thought I'd have to listen, hard,
I didn't even swallow.
But nothing from you stopped.

Isn't there something

Isn't there something in me
like the dogs I've heard at home
who bark all night from hunger? Something
in me like trains leaving,

isn't there something in me
like a gun? I wanted to be
loud squirrels, around the trees' feet,
bees, coming back & back

to the wooden porch,
wanting something—and wooden planks,
wanting something. To go back into
a tree?

I want to go back to you,
who when you were dying said
*There are one or two people you don't want to
let go of.* Here too, where I don't let go of you.

Down on the street

Down on the street
a man's voice, every night at ten—
God   God   God   I love you   God
Hallelujah   God
Hallelujah   God   God

Everyone breathing hard to get through,
to get through soon to the air,
a word in everybody's mouth—

You must have trusted some word
that time in that half-underwater cave
when you dove and came up someplace else,
and called to me, *Come on*

Both you & he

Both you & he were there.
I woke up, saw just you,
rumpled cloth hat, eyes closed.
I moved my head, and lost you.

Do I still need to disguise you
in my dream?

Oh north star, disguise what?
My friend,
I can still smell your clothes,
salt, light, the dog, and you.

My words to you

My words to you are the stitches in a scarf
I don't want to finish
maybe it will come to be a blanket
to hold you here

love not gone anywhere

I'm going to sleep

I'm going to sleep now
in case you visit my dream

Full moon   on your left temple
that nickel-size circle of whiter skin
under your straight black hair

I love it specially
as if it is my secret.
From before.

I'd get you a glass of champagne

      if we were still
in that hollow of sand and rock
above the beach. Talking by
listening. If you
were still breathing. *Our purpose
no-purpose.*

We turn in dream

We turn in dream
you to your place
me to mine.

        Across the street from each other
we both turn back,
you wait, short of breath.

I run back across the street,
you wait, your open jacket,
the cars are kind also, & wait.

                God

to be born
into no oxygen
then into breathing.

Are all the things

Are all the things that never happened, OK?
—The wide river at dawn, the hippo's lifted face
—The slow, violet curtains of Antarctic light
(Hide you under the shadow of their wings)

And all the things that came—
the awful, and then love on earth, OK?
my own friend?   where you are?

You're gone

You're gone in the day time
but you're still here at night

I'm going to sleep again
now, just in case

               not-God, not you quite, either, come
               —while underground,
your mother bites her wrist-vein
open, to let you drink.

Then

Then no friend, no you
under the subway light   no you

wanting a hand
asking anyone
"Can you help me to speak?"

You Speak

I'm not without you friend
but without stars,
skin & fingers, borders

not separated out. Here
you get past everything
all at once. I remember

everything. That white tree.
And what was never there
to remember, I remember

as if I've come upon
a whole room full of clay books
that I can read with my fingers,

as we once read each other,
younger than water, remember? And
"—if transformation comes?"

I could compare it maybe to a train
in Tolstoy, already having forgiven
everything, forward & backward:

                              the train is saying
Come on. I'm writing on a tablecloth.
I love you.

Threshold

Could it be heat?

Could it be heat? Could I be growing out? You my father
in a chair pulled up to the foot of my bed,
rubbing and rubbing my feet, under the blanket,

when I was eleven, when you came back from the war,
Sorry, you said, *I can't speak, it's,*
I'm dead. You rubbed my feet, a hundred years went by.

You sent me away to the library for love.
I found two books: the Window and the Door.
All I did was wait & sleep & write. *Please change. Please open.*

Another hundred years,
The Window opened me.
The Door said, *More.*

The Window:

Did you not suppose I loved you?
I loved you, asleep in the library,
your hair the hue of rain-drenched bark.

But I am little in that world of
home, of bed and chair.
I can't touch there, or see.

I jumped on the subway tracks
when I was seven, they said I fell,
I didn't fall.

They come toward me, a noise starts up
in my ears, an engine of air & kill.

       Can't you understand? I've loved—

—I've loved a woman before this,
in the Philippines, in the war, and then, another,
back here, since.

                         There is nothing to open.
Nothing to change.
Now do you understand?

I am a dead tree to the touch.
There is nothing to change.
There is nothing to open.

I love you more, then,
dead tree—you
who open whoever you approach;
you change the comer.

The last time I saw you, it was winter, your hand
held hard to my hand,   you asked
"How long are you here for?"
You bent toward me,

the change in your red lips was death,
cadmium red deep-painted mouth—

When you died, I dreamed
you had fallen asleep on the subway

—Not all that praise laid out on a teak tray
and offered to us to eat,   unhungry.

When I woke up
my clothes were covered with writing,
my hair was sentences, full of twigs,

lines ran between my fingers.
Open, Window, Look, it's
time to fly now.

The owl looked back to me a minute
from the sill: stiff feathers stood
around his eyes: his book.

The Door:

When I first heard you on the phone
your voice had to be that '40s wartime voice
for it to get under my skin like it did,
after seven years asleep.

You're at the beginning of something, you said,
and I'm at the end of something;
but you didn't go away,
twice-born, three times, coming around,
rough cello.

                    Late days
I want to drive to your grave,
But I don't belong to it.

Bellini, Saint Francis

The mountain rocks are blue-green.
The donkey is alone now.
And the crane.
And the rabbit. Next to the book,
the skull. Nothing darkens it.

I know you went blind.
I know you died.
Nothing darkens you, threshold.
Nothing lightens you. You
life unsustainable here   Just about

In the Famine Museum

Don't do that, my mother said,
when I went to put my arm
around her.

So, she said,
*you're only here
for a day or two.*

We are separate ashes
and bone covered over.
We have a mother, both—our
great-grandmother.
We sit with her
in the Famine Museum
—the begot life—arms
(I don't know how)
around each other's waists.

Great-grandmother, my mother says,
Come for a walk.

Cán the dead walk? she asks.

My mother answers,

—How not?

Friend,

you came in a dream yesterday
—The first day we met
you showed me your dark workroom
off the kitchen, your books, your notebooks.

Reading our last, knowing-last letters
—the years of our friendship
reading our poems to each other,
I would start breathing again.

Yesterday, in the afternoon,
more than a year since you died,

some words came into the air.
I looked away a second,
and they were gone—
six lines, just passing through.

for Adrienne Rich

Great-grandmother,

be with us
as if in the one same day & night
we all gave birth
in the one same safe-house, warm,
and then we rest together,
sleep, and nurse,
dreamily talk to our babies, warm
in a safe room   all of us
carried in the close black sky.

Then had we well put to,
without form, without text

ANTONIN ARTAUD

Note in winter

Clear window
for now. I,
human animal,
with heat,
& ceiling,
risk.

I gave you
some bad, worn memories.
I know you will not leave,

but risk.

The iron plow
scraping past.
And no snow.

Ten Degrees

From her sidewalk newspaper blanket
she asks for a sandwich,
as if from a mother.

The street has the white
look of winter.
The subways flood.

You have to think with water.

When I woke up, our time

When I woke up, our time was lost. No standing
in physics.   the unconscious.

I washed our friends' old rug
and laid it across the table.

Mandelstam,
the river was shining, silver as a plow.

Your friend, Natasha, the lame girl,
walking ahead, held back her hand
to you on the street:

     —Come on, I've got the rug—

And you said

*—Where did I put you
down dear? The world is worse
but I can hear your heart
so steady.   louder.*

Someone taken.   Beating a rug.

When I woke up, my friend

When I woke up, my friend
was there with me.
We were on the island
of no going beyond.

Why do they call the dead
the never-returners?

You brought vegetables up from the kitchen,
whistling to let me know
you were approaching the steps.

And even here
two days after you died
we talked on W. 17th Sreet—

Then everything complicated,
swift & gear.

Self-Portrait, Rembrandt, 1658

I can't look up out of the sadness
only here along with your sadness

In the line of your black hat   the line
around the crown of my head gets stronger
when people come & go between us

From the first time I saw you,
when I was young,
you held me in your own understanding exhaustion.

Song

I was asking pardon, who am I?
Of them who I am: pardon.

Of the slow wearing down
of the window, the sun, I was asking forgiveness,

of the crocodile, that good hider,
of the heron, that good feeder,

& of Christ the pelican.
                      Christ said,

Over a thousand pages of Scripture,
& I was not reading, but dreaming.

It's the same right now, he said.
                     He just stood there.

I, I was not painting, but watching the animals.
I was not copying, but dreaming.

Over one thousand newborns in this clearing. We started
to lick them clean, dreaming, one by one.

Icebergs, Ilulissat

In blue-green air & water God
you have come back for us,
to our fiberglass boat.

You have come back for us, & I'm afraid.
Great sadness at harms.
But nothing now
can be like before.

Even when the icebergs are gone, and the millions of suns
have burnt themselves out of your arms,

your arms of burnt air.

ACKNOWLEDGMENTS

The American Poetry Review

The Boston Review

Faultline

Field

Fifth Wednesday

Gwarlingo

Ibbetson Street Magazine

la petite zine

Little Star

Martha's Vineyard Arts and Ideas

Plume

St. Petersburg Review

Spacecraft

Spoon River Poetry Review

Deep thanks to Janet Kaplan of Red Glass Books for printing *The Ship* and to Brian Teare for printing *Friend* in Albion Books.

The poem *God of Rooms* was published in *Homage to Paul Celan*, edited by Ilya Kaminsky & G.C. Waldrep.

Deep thanks to Peter Shumann & the Bread & Puppet Theater for *Shirt in Heaven*, the masonite-cut on the cover, and also for the book's title.

With heartfelt gratitude to everyone at the Lannan Foundation, the MacDowell Colony, VCCA, Vermont Studio Center, to Jaime Shearn Coan, and to the horses.

About the Author

Jean Valentine is the author of twelve books of poetry, and has taught at Sarah Lawrence College, New York University, and the 92nd St. YM-YWHA. A collection of her poetry, *Door in the Mountain,* won the National Book Award in 2004. With the poet Ilya Kaminsky she translated some poetry and prose by Marina Tsvetaeva, *Dark Elderberry Branch.* Valentine has also edited a book of essays on the poetry of Eleanor Ross Taylor, *The Lighthouse Keeper.* She lives in New York City.

Poetry is vital to language and living. Since 1972, Copper Canyon Press has published extraordinary poetry from around the world to engage the imaginations and intellects of readers, writers, booksellers, librarians, teachers, students, and donors.

WE ARE GRATEFUL FOR THE MAJOR SUPPORT PROVIDED BY:

THE PAUL G. ALLEN
FAMILY FOUNDATION

Lannan

WE ARE GRATEFUL FOR THE MAJOR SUPPORT PROVIDED BY:

Anonymous

John Branch

Diana Broze

Beroz Ferrell & The Point, LLC

Janet and Les Cox

Mimi Gardner Gates

Linda Gerrard and Walter Parsons

Gull Industries, Inc.
on behalf of William and Ruth True

Mark Hamilton and Suzie Rapp

Carolyn and Robert Hedin

Steven Myron Holl

Lakeside Industries, Inc.
on behalf of Jeanne Marie Lee

Maureen Lee and Mark Busto

Brice Marden

Ellie Mathews and Carl Youngmann
as The North Press

H. Stewart Parker

Penny and Jerry Peabody

John Phillips and Anne O'Donnell

Joseph C. Roberts

Cynthia Lovelace Sears and
Frank Buxton

The Seattle Foundation

Kim and Jeff Seely

David and Catherine Eaton Skinner

Dan Waggoner

C.D. Wright and Forrest Gander

Charles and Barbara Wright

The dedicated interns and faithful volunteers
of Copper Canyon Press

~~~~~

TO LEARN MORE ABOUT UNDERWRITING COPPER CANYON PRESS TITLES,
PLEASE CALL 360-385-4925 EXT. 103

The Chinese character for poetry is made up of two parts: "word" and "temple." It also serves as pressmark for Copper Canyon Press.

This book is set in Whitman, developed from Kent Lew's studies of W.A. Dwiggins's Caledonia. Titles set in Filosofia, designed by Zuzana Ličko. Book design and composition by VJB/Scribe. Printed on archival-quality paper.